THE HAPPY BODY

Virtues

Daily Practices for the Modern Stoic

ALSO BY ANIELA AND JERZY GREGOREK

Non-Fiction
The Happy Body (2009)
I Got This: The Art of Getting Grit (2016)
Self Mastery Workbook (2017)

Poetry
Sacred and Scared (2014)
Food for Your Soul (2014)
Locket: A Mother in the World (2016)
Family Tree (2018)

Dialogues
The Happy Body: Mastering Food Choices (2015)
The Happy Body: Mastering Exercise Choices (2015)
The Happy Body: Mastering Rest Choices (2015)

Translations
Late Confession by Józef Baran (1997)
Watermarks by Bogusław Żurakowski (2000)
Her Miniature by Zbigniew Czuchajowski (2000)
In a Flash by Józef Baran (2000)
The Poetry of Maurycy Szymel (2004)
The Shy Hand of a Jew by Maurycy (Mosze) Szymel (2013)
Native Foreigners: Jewish–Polish Poetry Between the World Wars (2015)

CD
Food for Your Soul (2013)

Videos
The Happy Body Ambience (2013)
The Happy Body Exercise Program (2014)

THE HAPPY BODY

Virtues

Daily Practices for the Modern Stoic

by

Aniela & Jerzy Gregorek

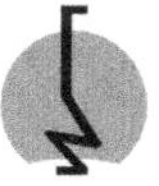

The Happy Body Press
Woodside, California
2019

We dedicate this book to Jerzy Popieluszko

Truth, Love, and Forgiveness

CONTENTS

INTRODUCTION

toics saw happiness as flow in life, a combination of self-control and virtue. To be virtuous was to live life without waste and work toward perfecting yourself, not only physically but also intellectually. Wisdom was in recognizing where you have control in life, and how to achieve smooth progress with small increments, what we call in The Happy Body, "micro-progression." Wisdom also lay in recognizing where you don't have control and learning to let go.

The Happy Body Program was developed with the same principles in mind. In three areas of our daily lifestyle practice we have a choice: food (what to eat, how much and when); exercise (the kind that will benefit our body over time and keep it healthy and fit), restoration of our body (with well-timed meditation or relaxation practice). By setting high standards and making hard choices to achieve them, you're becoming more virtuous. Socrates, one of the most famous Stoics, advised that we should eat to live and not live to eat. He taught his students that whenever we eat too much or drink when not thirsty, it weakens our character. He advised that we should take charge of our health and learn from professionals how to keep the body healthy, also learning from our own experiences what food or exercise makes bodies feel good.

Over the years we've learned from our practitioners that the right words at the right time for the right person can work magic. These virtuous sayings were created spontaneously with clients at times when the connection was powerful and we were in a heightened, intuitive state. The words were a catalyst; our practitioners could suddenly understand and embrace what they hadn't before. They shifted. They had a new feeling.

A year will pass, let this one flow smoothly as you accumulate virtue, self-control and happiness.

HOW TO USE THIS BOOK

There are 52 virtuous precepts in this book, along with seven prompts for daily reflection for each day of the week to encourage deep practice. A model follows, illustrating how working with these prompts can help you integrate the precepts on intellectual, feeling, spiritual, and practical levels.

First read the precept, then turn the page to read a short explication. On the facing page you will work with the precept each day of the week, approaching it from a variety of angles to better understand and embody its wisdom.

The first four days are based on interior reflection and knowledge; the last three days involve the active practice of building the skill of the virtue through planning, strategy and experience. Only by applying the wisdom to act in the real world will it truly become a consistent behavior in your life.

Hard Choices, Easy Life.
Easy Choices, Hard Life.

*When we choose the more difficult options that life presents,
it means that we are stepping onto a path that will make us better
over time. And our life eventually becomes easier.*

Day 1: I understand that getting better is always tough work. I won't change without making an effort.

Day 2: I think I've been oblivious to all the ways I've taken the easy way out in the past. I didn't grow up with much discipline, so now I see it's something I need to work on and teach myself.

Day 3: I feel overwhelmed by what is required to simply get better. I feel like giving up my evening cookies will be hard. I already resent that I have to control my portions.

Day 4: I believe it is possible. I know other people who were successful, so I can be too. I believe that I can do this if I just keep at it.

Day 5: My plan is stick to the three-hour eating schedule, making sure I never skip a snack so I don't get too hungry and then overeat.

Day 6: My strategy is to first clean out the fridge and cabinets, removing all temptations and foods that aren't on the plan. I will stock up on healthy foods I really like, and prepare snacks ahead of time so I can grab them quickly if I'm rushed.

Day 7: My experience is that it's hard to stick with the rigid schedule. Sometimes I'm hungry before the time or I'm not hungry when it's time to eat. I miss my cookies. But I also feel reassured that I do get to eat frequently. I won't starve on this plan and I know it's healthy.

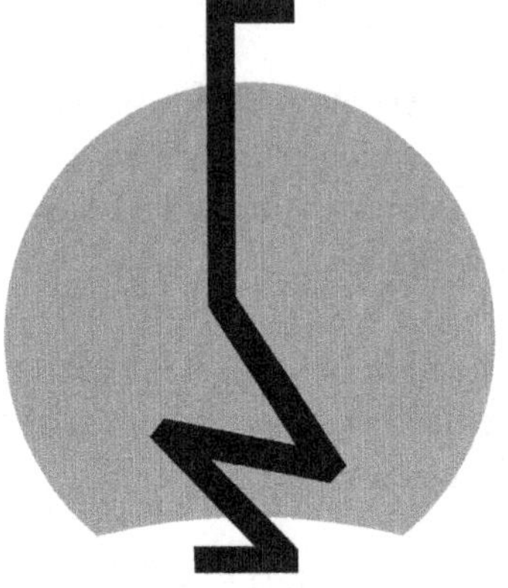

No choice, no freedom.

If you feel that you are already defined—
by your habits, culture, education, family—
your identity is the invisible chain that binds you.

WEEK 1

Day 1: I understand _______________________________
____
____

Day 2: I think ___________________________________
____
____

Day 3: I feel ____________________________________
____
____

Day 4: I believe _________________________________
____
____

Day 5: My plan is ________________________________
____
____

Day 6: My strategy is _____________________________
____
____

Day 7: My experience is ___________________________
____
____

Failure needs forgiveness.

*Dwelling on past mistakes robs you of energy for
new opportunities. Why live in a negative space when you can free
yourself by taking ownership of the present and restarting?*

WEEK 2

Day 1: I understand _______________________________
____
____

Day 2: I think ___________________________________
____
____

Day 3: I feel ____________________________________
____
____

Day 4: I believe _________________________________
____
____

Day 5: My plan is ________________________________
____
____

Day 6: My strategy is ____________________________
____
____

Day 7: My experience is __________________________
____
____

Not improving is normal; becoming human is abnormal.

Many people follow a predictable script for life without testing their limits. Once you activate the part of you that seeks challenge and self-improvement, you're on the way to discovering your true human potential.

WEEK 3

Day 1: I understand _______________________

____

____

Day 2: I think _______________________

____

____

Day 3: I feel _______________________

____

____

Day 4: I believe _______________________

____

____

Day 5: My plan is _______________________

____

____

Day 6: My strategy is _______________________

____

____

Day 7: My experience is _______________________

____

____

Mastery is in the details.

Knowledge of how to calibrate the accumulation of new behavior to adapt to a new level is essential in the process of achieving significant goals.

WEEK 4

Day 1: I understand ______________________________
____
____

Day 2: I think ________________________________
____
____

Day 3: I feel _________________________________
____
____

Day 4: I believe ______________________________
____
____

Day 5: My plan is _____________________________
____
____

Day 6: My strategy is __________________________
____
____

Day 7: My experience is ________________________
____
____

You never "forget yourself."

*The moment you shirk responsibility for negative prior action,
you're dooming yourself to repeat it. Awareness of how
your fatalist works can break the pattern.*

WEEK 5

Day 1: I understand _______________________________
____
____

Day 2: I think _________________________________
____
____

Day 3: I feel _________________________________
____
____

Day 4: I believe _______________________________
____
____

Day 5: My plan is ______________________________
____
____

Day 6: My strategy is ___________________________
____
____

Day 7: My experience is _________________________
____
____

Controlling yourself is attractive.
Controlling others is repulsive.
Helping others to control themselves is magical.

We all strive to be the best version of ourselves; this can only come through self-control. Helping others to acquire this skill is the highest form of service. It is the key to personal independence and flourishing communities.

Day 1: I understand _______________________________

____

____

Day 2: I think ___________________________________

____

____

Day 3: I feel ____________________________________

____

____

Day 4: I believe _________________________________

____

____

Day 5: My plan is _________________________________

____

____

Day 6: My strategy is _____________________________

____

____

Day 7: My experience is ___________________________

____

____

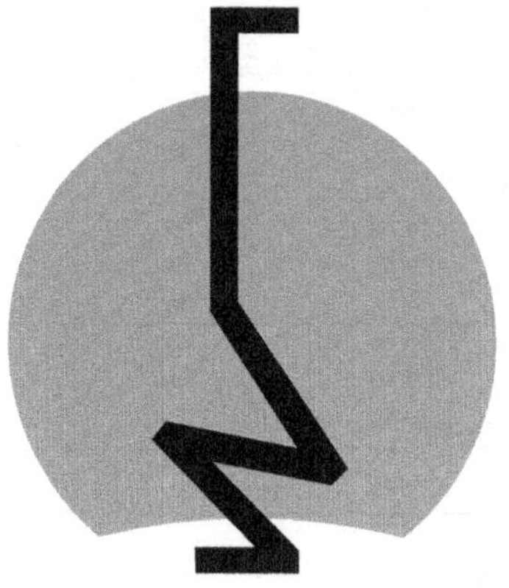

Knowledge doesn't develop skill; action does.

*What if you read 100 books to help yourself lose weight and
you still didn't lose it? You are tested in life by doing. No matter how
much knowledge you acquire, nothing happens until you
take action that develops skill.*

WEEK 7

Day 1: I understand _______________________________________

____

____

Day 2: I think ____

____

____

Day 3: I feel ____

____

____

Day 4: I believe _______________________________________

____

____

Day 5: My plan is ______________________________________

____

____

Day 6: My strategy is ___________________________________

____

____

Day 7: My experience is _________________________________

____

____

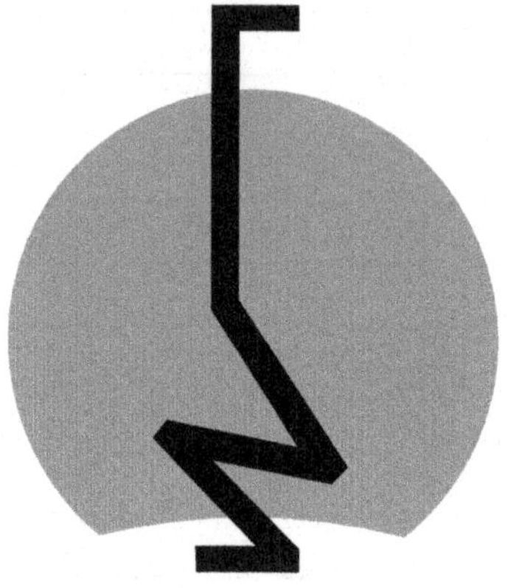

Variety kills quality.

The endless search for novelty or entertainment distracts you from mastering what matters.

WEEK 8

Day 1: I understand _______________________________

____

____

Day 2: I think _______________________________

____

____

Day 3: I feel _______________________________

____

____

Day 4: I believe _______________________________

____

____

Day 5: My plan is _______________________________

____

____

Day 6: My strategy is _______________________________

____

____

Day 7: My experience is _______________________________

____

____

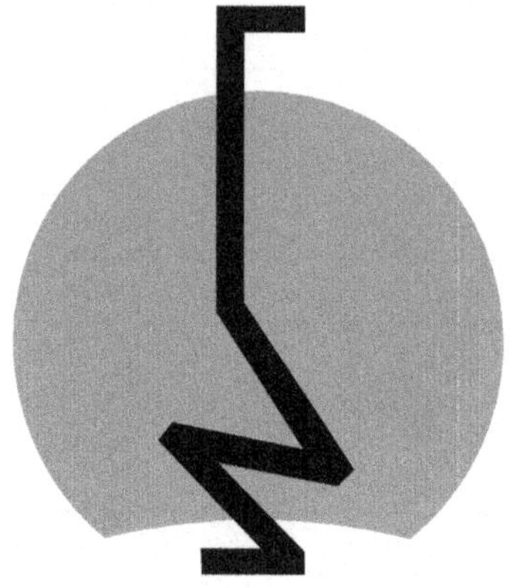

Master Chooses, Fatalist Loses.

Life is like a seesaw, with a constant tipping point between what you are and what you can be. If you constantly tilt in the direction of the Master, eventually you'll become one.

WEEK 9

Day 1: I understand ______________________

____

____

Day 2: I think ______________________

____

____

Day 3: I feel ______________________

____

____

Day 4: I believe ______________________

____

____

Day 5: My plan is ______________________

____

____

Day 6: My strategy is ______________________

____

____

Day 7: My experience is ______________________

____

____

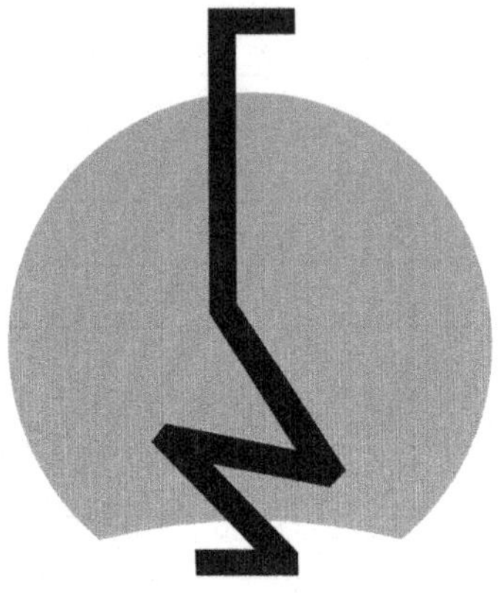

Be the right thing.

Goodness lies in challenging yourself, especially when it is difficult. These are the moments when you are tested to live up to your own ideals.

WEEK 10

Day 1: I understand _______________________________

____

____

Day 2: I think _______________________________

____

____

Day 3: I feel _______________________________

____

____

Day 4: I believe _______________________________

____

____

Day 5: My plan is _______________________________

____

____

Day 6: My strategy is _______________________________

____

____

Day 7: My experience is _______________________________

____

____

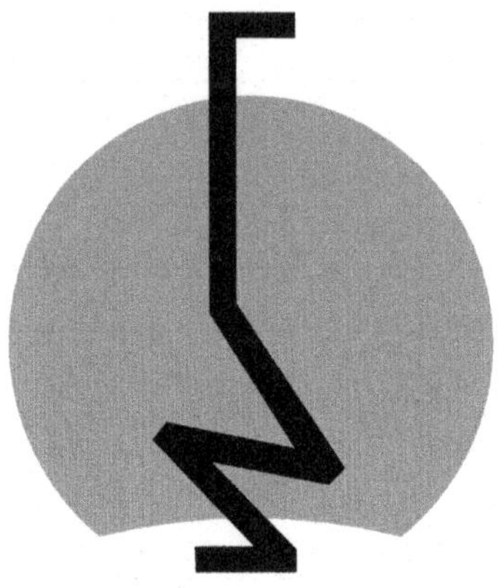

Depression belongs to you; you can disown it.

In spite of what brought you to this state (genetics, trauma, misfortune), the moment you realize that you are the one who must choose to climb out is the moment of refusal and liberation.

WEEK 11

Day 1: I understand ____

____

____

Day 2: I think ____

____

____

Day 3: I feel ____

____

____

Day 4: I believe ____

____

____

Day 5: My plan is ____

____

____

Day 6: My strategy is _____________________________________

____

____

Day 7: My experience is ___________________________________

____

____

Stress doesn't exist.

*Only your response to a potentially stressful situation does.
If two people can respond differently to the same situation, then it's
the attitude that matters; this is a choice.*

WEEK 12

Day 1: I understand ________________________________

____

____

Day 2: I think ___________________________________

____

____

Day 3: I feel ____________________________________

____

____

Day 4: I believe __________________________________

____

____

Day 5: My plan is ________________________________

____

____

Day 6: My strategy is _____________________________

____

____

Day 7: My experience is ____________________________

____

____

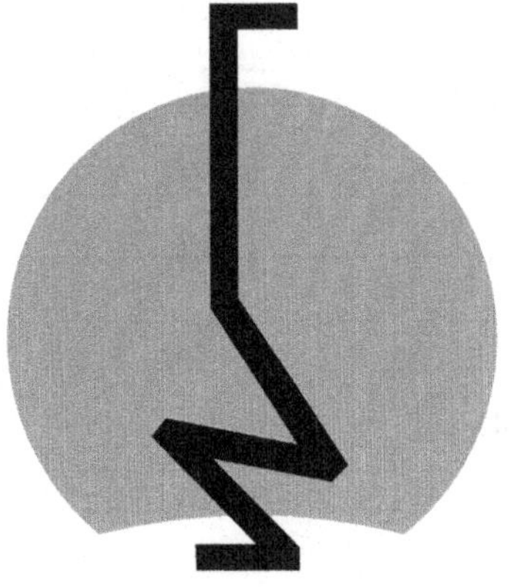

Commit to the unlikable but virtuous act.

The ultimate wisdom is to fall in love with what we don't like but is good for us.

WEEK 13

Day 1: I understand ______________________________

____

____

Day 2: I think __________________________________

____

____

Day 3: I feel ____________________________________

____

____

Day 4: I believe ________________________________

____

____

Day 5: My plan is ________________________________

____

____

Day 6: My strategy is ____________________________

____

____

Day 7: My experience is __________________________

____

____

My anger is mine.

No one has the power to "make" you angry. Blaming others for your emotion diminishes your own power to manage it.

WEEK 14

Day 1: I understand _______________________________

____

____

Day 2: I think _______________________________

____

____

Day 3: I feel _______________________________

____

____

Day 4: I believe _______________________________

____

____

Day 5: My plan is _______________________________

____

____

Day 6: My strategy is _______________________________

____

____

Day 7: My experience is _______________________________

____

____

"Delicious" food doesn't exist.

Someone may love one food, while another will find it distasteful. Taste is conditioned by culture and you can change your conditioning.

WEEK 15

Day 1: I understand _______________________________
____
____

Day 2: I think _______________________________
____
____

Day 3: I feel _______________________________
____
____

Day 4: I believe _______________________________
____
____

Day 5: My plan is _______________________________
____
____

Day 6: My strategy is _______________________________
____
____

Day 7: My experience is _______________________________
____
____

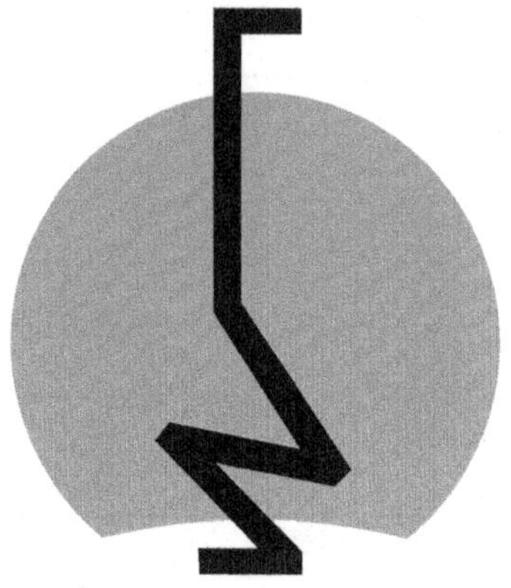

The body is at the mercy of the mind.

The body is vulnerable and has no agency on its own.
The mind determines how it will be.

WEEK 16

Day 1: I understand ______________________
____
____

Day 2: I think ____________________________
____
____

Day 3: I feel _____________________________
____
____

Day 4: I believe __________________________
____
____

Day 5: My plan is _________________________
____
____

Day 6: My strategy is ______________________
____
____

Day 7: My experience is ____________________
____
____

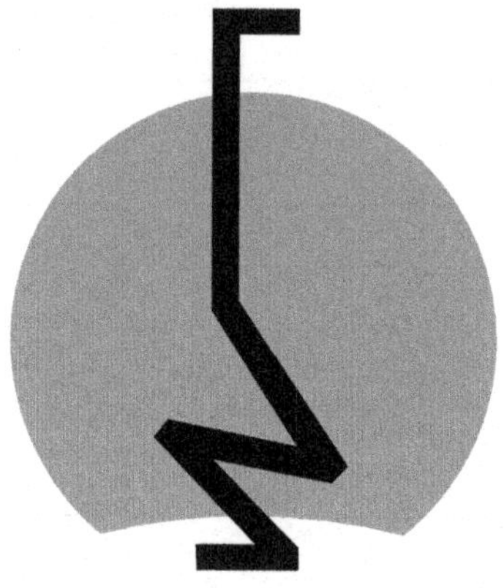

The body does speak; it also has the last word.

*The mind can overwork and abuse the body, but the body's physical
limitations will remind you when you've gone too far.
The first sign is pain—if not heeded, injury is unavoidable.*

WEEK 17

Day 1: I understand _______________________________
____
____

Day 2: I think _______________________________
____
____

Day 3: I feel _______________________________
____
____

Day 4: I believe _______________________________
____
____

Day 5: My plan is _______________________________
____
____

Day 6: My strategy is _______________________________
____
____

Day 7: My experience is _______________________________
____
____

The body doesn't resist change, the mind does.

If you can change your mind-based habits, you can achieve the desired results in the body.

WEEK 18

Day 1: I understand ________________________________

____

____

Day 2: I think ________________________________

____

____

Day 3: I feel ________________________________

____

____

Day 4: I believe ________________________________

____

____

Day 5: My plan is ________________________________

____

____

Day 6: My strategy is ________________________________

____

____

Day 7: My experience is ________________________________

____

____

Knowledge can be deceptive.

If you know how to get fat, does it mean you know how to get lean?
And if you know how to get lean, does it mean you are lean?

WEEK 19

Day 1: I understand ____

____

____

Day 2: I think ____

____

____

Day 3: I feel ____

____

____

Day 4: I believe ____

____

____

Day 5: My plan is ____

____

____

Day 6: My strategy is _______________________________________

____

____

Day 7: My experience is _____________________________________

____

____

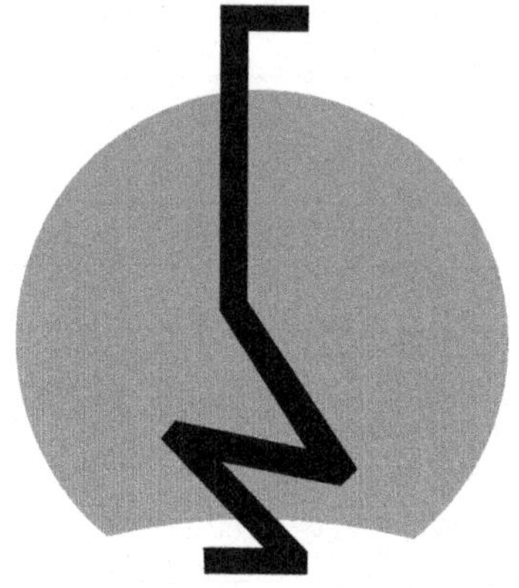

Pursuit is not attainment.

*You need concrete, measurable goals, along with a strategy
and a plan to reach them.*

WEEK 20

Day 1: I understand _________________________

____

____

Day 2: I think _________________________

____

____

Day 3: I feel _________________________

____

____

Day 4: I believe _________________________

____

____

Day 5: My plan is _________________________

____

____

Day 6: My strategy is _________________________

____

____

Day 7: My experience is _________________________

____

____

Excellence is never instantaneous.

If you rush, you'll never get there.

WEEK 21

Day 1: I understand ___________________________________

____

____

Day 2: I think ___________________________________

____

____

Day 3: I feel ___________________________________

____

____

Day 4: I believe ___________________________________

____

____

Day 5: My plan is ___________________________________

____

____

Day 6: My strategy is ___________________________________

____

____

Day 7: My experience is ___________________________________

____

____

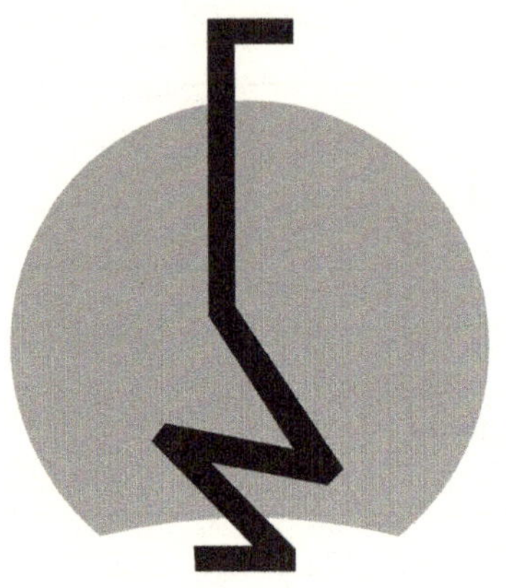

The Fatalist loves vagueness.

The Master loves clarity.
The Master's power lies in knowing and being responsible for results, whereas the Fatalist thrives on procrastination, invisibility, and slippery avoidance of the work required for achievement.

WEEK 22

Day 1: I understand _________________________________
____
____

Day 2: I think _____________________________________
____
____

Day 3: I feel ______________________________________
____
____

Day 4: I believe ___________________________________
____
____

Day 5: My plan is ___________________________________
____
____

Day 6: My strategy is _________________________________
____
____

Day 7: My experience is _______________________________
____
____

Standards should always be high.

Motivating yourself to become someone you've never been before initiates an awakening that helps you to withstand discomfort.

WEEK 23

Day 1: I understand _______________________

____

____

Day 2: I think _______________________

____

____

Day 3: I feel _______________________

____

____

Day 4: I believe _______________________

____

____

Day 5: My plan is _______________________

____

____

Day 6: My strategy is _______________________

____

____

Day 7: My experience is _______________________

____

____

Over-talkers underperform.

Don't indulge yourself with words.

WEEK 24

Day 1: I understand _______________________________

____

____

Day 2: I think ___________________________________

____

____

Day 3: I feel ____________________________________

____

____

Day 4: I believe _________________________________

____

____

Day 5: My plan is ________________________________

____

____

Day 6: My strategy is _____________________________

____

____

Day 7: My experience is ___________________________

____

____

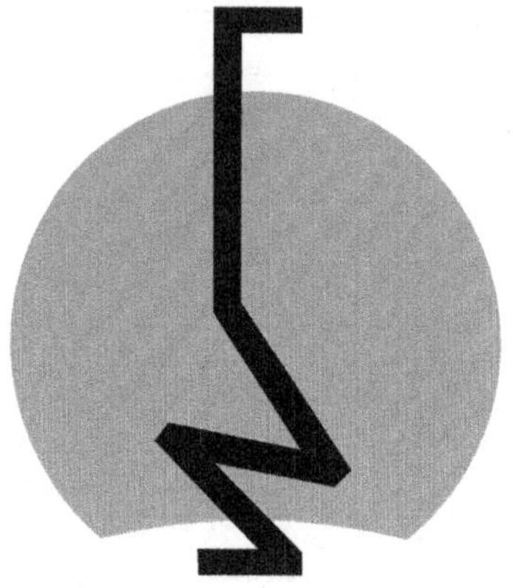

Winners celebrate; losers talk.

Winning is just the pinnacle of all the work and preparation you've already put in. Lack of achievement is often covered up with excess explanation.

WEEK 25

Day 1: I understand ________________________________

____

____

Day 2: I think ___________________________________

____

____

Day 3: I feel ____________________________________

____

____

Day 4: I believe _________________________________

____

____

Day 5: My plan is ________________________________

____

____

Day 6: My strategy is _____________________________

____

____

Day 7: My experience is ___________________________

____

____

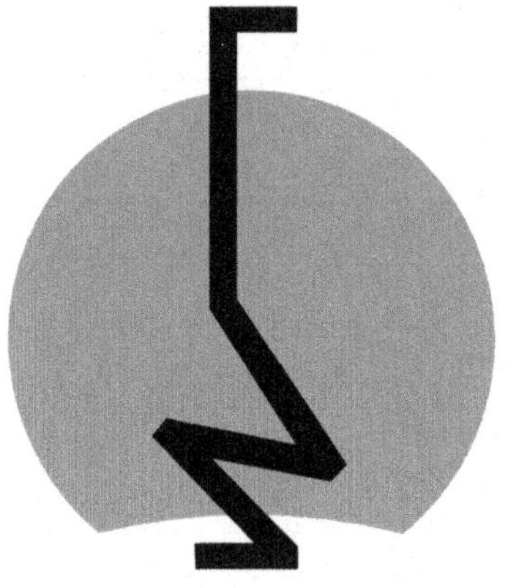

116

You are your memories.

What will your new memories be? Choosing to initiate action gives you your identity.

WEEK 26

Day 1: I understand _______________________________

____

____

Day 2: I think ___________________________________

____

____

Day 3: I feel ____________________________________

____

____

Day 4: I believe _________________________________

____

____

Day 5: My plan is ________________________________

____

____

Day 6: My strategy is _____________________________

____

____

Day 7: My experience is ___________________________

____

____

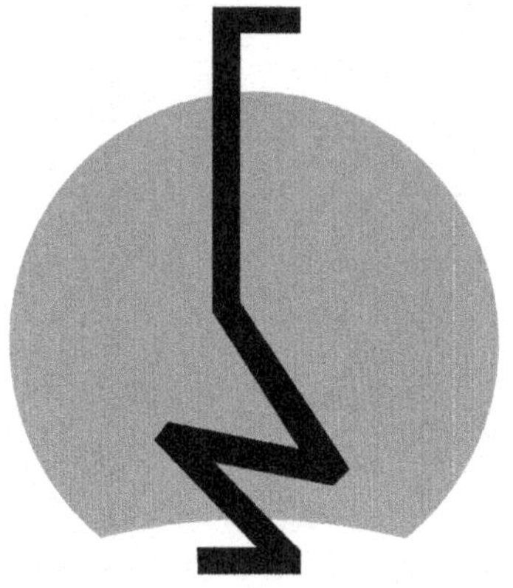

Language makes us human.

*We define and reveal ourselves with our words.
We must choose them with care.*

WEEK 27

Day 1: I understand _______________________________

____

____

Day 2: I think ___________________________________

____

____

Day 3: I feel ____________________________________

____

____

Day 4: I believe _________________________________

____

____

Day 5: My plan is ________________________________

____

____

Day 6: My strategy is ____________________________

____

____

Day 7: My experience is __________________________

____

____

Stoicism is not revolutionary, being a stoic is.

No one can control you if you control yourself.

WEEK 28

Day 1: I understand ___________________________

____

____

Day 2: I think ___________________________

____

____

Day 3: I feel ___________________________

____

____

Day 4: I believe ___________________________

____

____

Day 5: My plan is ___________________________

____

____

Day 6: My strategy is ___________________________

____

____

Day 7: My experience is ___________________________

____

____

Today is not yet finished.

You still have time to add to a better future.
I just did.
The Master can take charge in every moment.

WEEK 29

Day 1: I understand _______________________
____
____

Day 2: I think _______________________
____
____

Day 3: I feel _______________________
____
____

Day 4: I believe _______________________
____
____

Day 5: My plan is _______________________
____
____

Day 6: My strategy is _______________________
____
____

Day 7: My experience is _______________________
____
____

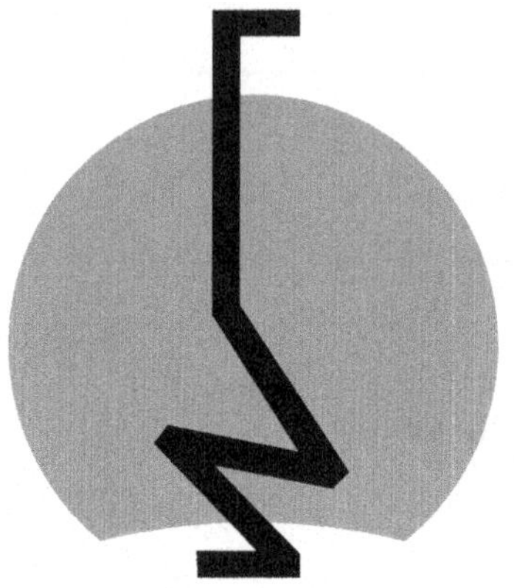

It's time.

You know what this means. Start fighting.

WEEK 30

Day 1: I understand _______________________________

____

____

Day 2: I think _______________________________

____

____

Day 3: I feel _______________________________

____

____

Day 4: I believe _______________________________

____

____

Day 5: My plan is _______________________________

____

____

Day 6: My strategy is _______________________________

____

____

Day 7: My experience is _______________________________

____

____

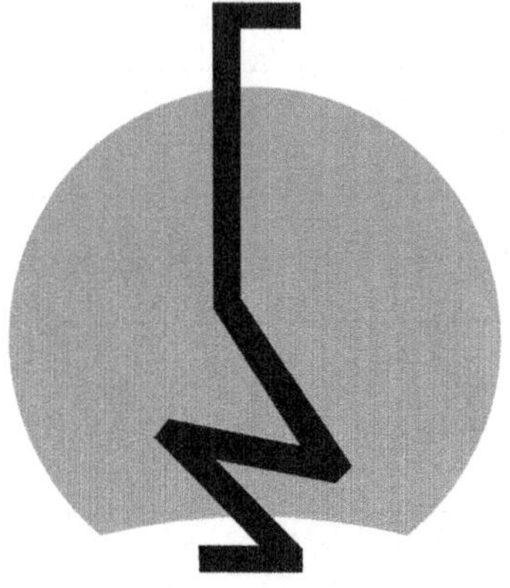

You will never have enough of something
you don't want in the first place.

Excess doesn't fulfill, it destroys.

WEEK 31

Day 1: I understand _______________________________

____

____

Day 2: I think _____________________________________

____

____

Day 3: I feel ______________________________________

____

____

Day 4: I believe ___________________________________

____

____

Day 5: My plan is __________________________________

____

____

Day 6: My strategy is ______________________________

____

____

Day 7: My experience is ____________________________

____

____

There's no "last time"—this is the time.

Maintaining ties to past habits prevents you from making the decisions that will improve your quality of life.

WEEK 32

Day 1: I understand ___________________________
____
____

Day 2: I think ___________________________
____
____

Day 3: I feel ___________________________
____
____

Day 4: I believe ___________________________
____
____

Day 5: My plan is ___________________________
____
____

Day 6: My strategy is ___________________________
____
____

Day 7: My experience is ___________________________
____
____

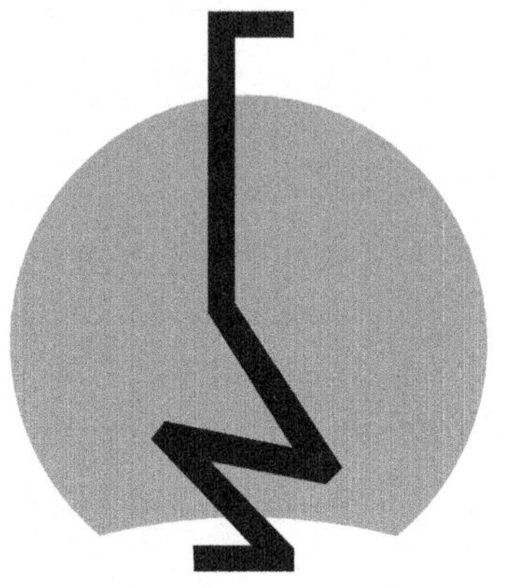

The future exists only in the past.

What you focus on in the present matters.
You only control the future that becomes the past
through present actions.

WEEK 33

Day 1: I understand _______________________
____
____

Day 2: I think _______________________
____
____

Day 3: I feel _______________________
____
____

Day 4: I believe _______________________
____
____

Day 5: My plan is _______________________
____
____

Day 6: My strategy is _______________________
____
____

Day 7: My experience is _______________________
____
____

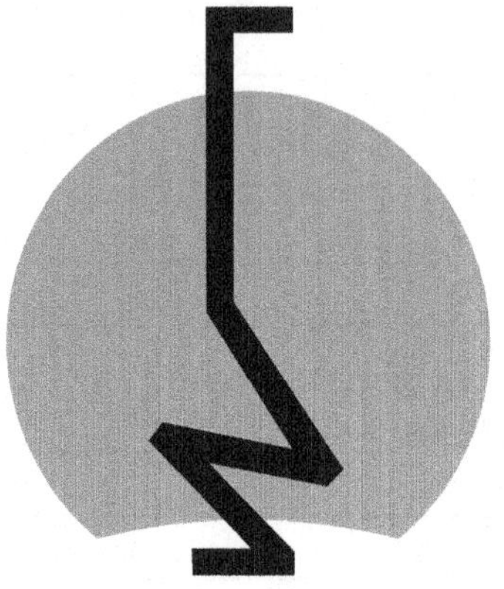

Micro-progression is unstoppable.

Over time, small changes create great outcomes.

WEEK 34

Day 1: I understand _______________________________

____

____

Day 2: I think _______________________________

____

____

Day 3: I feel _______________________________

____

____

Day 4: I believe _______________________________

____

____

Day 5: My plan is _______________________________

____

____

Day 6: My strategy is _______________________________

____

____

Day 7: My experience is _______________________________

____

____

You cannot "buy" good people.

You have to become a good person to attract good people.

WEEK 35

Day 1: I understand _____________________________

____

____

Day 2: I think ________________________________

____

____

Day 3: I feel _________________________________

____

____

Day 4: I believe ______________________________

____

____

Day 5: My plan is ______________________________

____

____

Day 6: My strategy is ___________________________

____

____

Day 7: My experience is _________________________

____

____

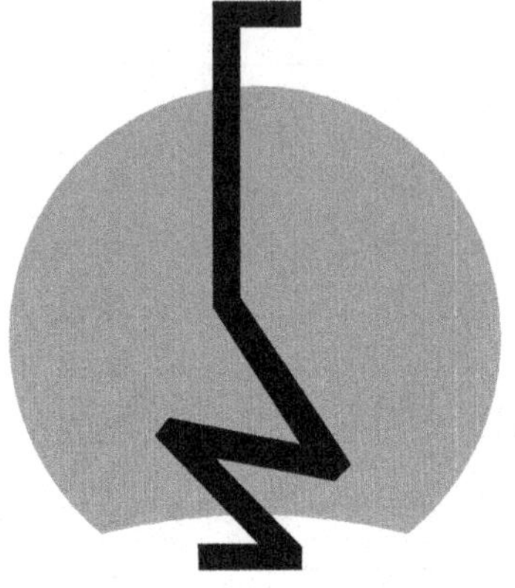

There's consistency in inconsistency.

*If you find yourself getting stuck, look for the pattern that shows
where you stray from the plan.*

WEEK 36

Day 1: I understand _______________________________

____

____

Day 2: I think _______________________________

____

____

Day 3: I feel _______________________________

____

____

Day 4: I believe _______________________________

____

____

Day 5: My plan is _______________________________

____

____

Day 6: My strategy is _______________________________

____

____

Day 7: My experience is _______________________________

____

____

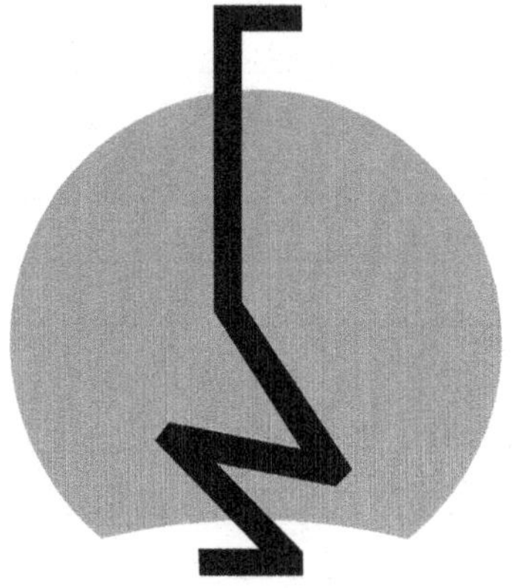

Two years will pass.

What we do with our time has cumulative results.

WEEK 37

Day 1: I understand _______________________________

____

____

Day 2: I think _______________________________

____

____

Day 3: I feel _______________________________

____

____

Day 4: I believe _______________________________

____

____

Day 5: My plan is _______________________________

____

____

Day 6: My strategy is _______________________________

____

____

Day 7: My experience is _______________________________

____

____

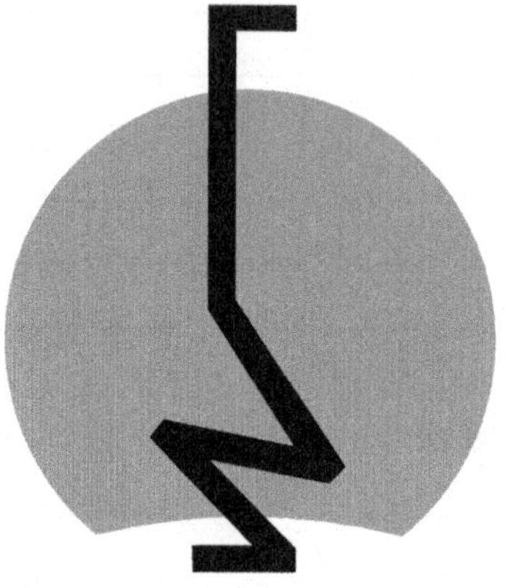

Regret is a trap.

*Dwelling on what can't be changed prevents you from
choosing a better present.*

WEEK 38

Day 1: I understand _______________________________

____

____

Day 2: I think _______________________________

____

____

Day 3: I feel _______________________________

____

____

Day 4: I believe _______________________________

____

____

Day 5: My plan is _______________________________

____

____

Day 6: My strategy is _______________________________

____

____

Day 7: My experience is _______________________________

____

____

You're always on time.

*Time doesn't change, but you can. It's never too early or
too late to create change.*

WEEK 39

Day 1: I understand _______________________________

____

____

Day 2: I think _______________________________

____

____

Day 3: I feel _______________________________

____

____

Day 4: I believe _______________________________

____

____

Day 5: My plan is _______________________________

____

____

Day 6: My strategy is _______________________________

____

____

Day 7: My experience is _______________________________

____

____

Discipline can be destructive.

Discipline is not an end in itself; it can be harnessed in the wrong pursuit.

WEEK 40

Day 1: I understand __________________________________

____

____

Day 2: I think ______________________________________

____

____

Day 3: I feel ____

____

____

Day 4: I believe ____________________________________

____

____

Day 5: My plan is ____________________________________

____

____

Day 6: My strategy is ________________________________

____

____

Day 7: My experience is ______________________________

____

____

A mentor is an illuminator.

*Sometimes we are blessed and mentors just appear. But sometimes
we hear the call and we must seek them out for ourselves.*

WEEK 41

Day 1: I understand _______________________________
____
____

Day 2: I think ___________________________________
____
____

Day 3: I feel ____________________________________
____
____

Day 4: I believe _________________________________
____
____

Day 5: My plan is ________________________________
____
____

Day 6: My strategy is ____________________________
____
____

Day 7: My experience is __________________________
____
____

Let Beginner's Mind be your home base.

*Frustration is the first sign that you've strayed from
the work you intended to accomplish.*

WEEK 42

Day 1: I understand _______________________

____

____

Day 2: I think _______________________

____

____

Day 3: I feel _______________________

____

____

Day 4: I believe _______________________

____

____

Day 5: My plan is _______________________

____

____

Day 6: My strategy is _______________________

____

____

Day 7: My experience is _______________________

____

____

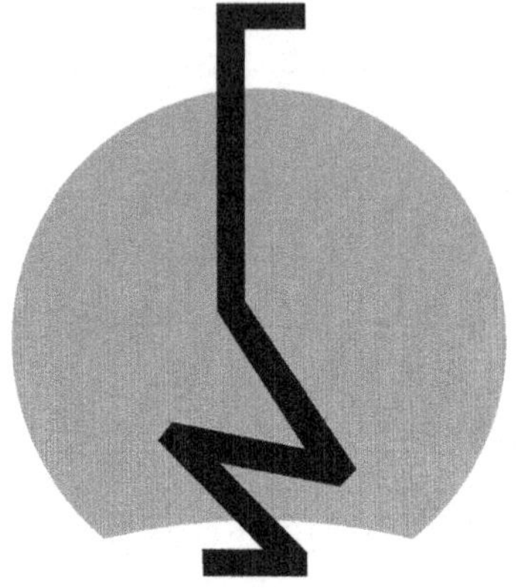

Self-control is more pleasurable than self-indulgence.

Giving into temptation ultimately creates disappointment and anxiety. On the other hand, delaying gratification nourishes self-worth and calmness.

WEEK 43

Day 1: I understand _______________________________
____
____

Day 2: I think _______________________________
____
____

Day 3: I feel _______________________________
____
____

Day 4: I believe _______________________________
____
____

Day 5: My plan is _______________________________
____
____

Day 6: My strategy is _______________________________
____
____

Day 7: My experience is _______________________________
____
____

Everything works.

Our actions bring results. It's no mystery that what you cultivate manifests in your world.

WEEK 44

Day 1: I understand ______________________________

____

____

Day 2: I think ______________________________

____

____

Day 3: I feel ______________________________

____

____

Day 4: I believe ______________________________

____

____

Day 5: My plan is ______________________________

____

____

Day 6: My strategy is ______________________________

____

____

Day 7: My experience is ______________________________

____

____

Don't let kindness be double-edged.

Kindness isn't kindness at all if expectations are attached.

WEEK 45

Day 1: I understand ______________________________

____

____

Day 2: I think ___________________________________

____

____

Day 3: I feel ____________________________________

____

____

Day 4: I believe _________________________________

____

____

Day 5: My plan is ________________________________

____

____

Day 6: My strategy is _____________________________

____

____

Day 7: My experience is ___________________________

____

____

No expectations, no disappointments.

*Expectations are a trap that stifles contentment
and our ability to flow.*

WEEK 46

Day 1: I understand _______________________

____

____

Day 2: I think _______________________

____

____

Day 3: I feel _______________________

____

____

Day 4: I believe _______________________

____

____

Day 5: My plan is _______________________

____

____

Day 6: My strategy is _______________________

____

____

Day 7: My experience is _______________________

____

____

Philosophize to live, or live to philosophize?

WEEK 47

Day 1: I understand _______________________

____

____

Day 2: I think _______________________

____

____

Day 3: I feel _______________________

____

____

Day 4: I believe _______________________

____

____

Day 5: My plan is _______________________

____

____

Day 6: My strategy is _______________________

____

____

Day 7: My experience is _______________________

____

____

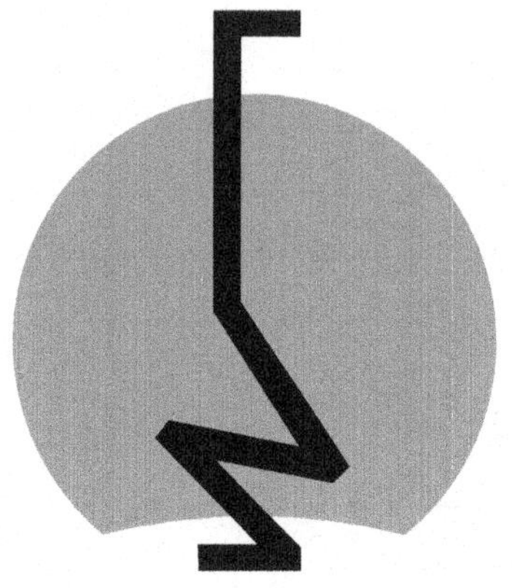

Minimize your exposure to impulse.

*Create a lifestyle that prevents the need to resist temptation.
Your capacity for resisting urges is finite, so you must create a
simplified environment where you can maintain control.*

WEEK 48

Day 1: I understand _______________________

____

____

Day 2: I think _______________________

____

____

Day 3: I feel _______________________

____

____

Day 4: I believe _______________________

____

____

Day 5: My plan is _______________________

____

____

Day 6: My strategy is _______________________

____

____

Day 7: My experience is _______________________

____

____

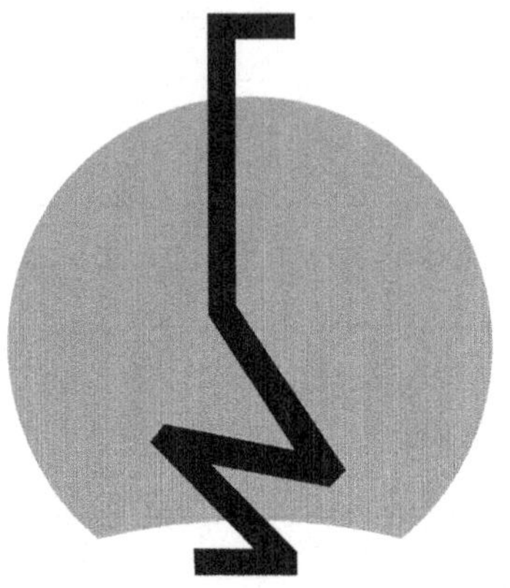

When your body acts out, you don't have to give in.

Automatic physiological responses, like blushing or increased heartbeat, do not have to escalate into negative emotions like shame or anger. Primitive physiological symptoms can be mastered so they have little impact on our everyday life.

WEEK 49

Day 1: I understand ______________________________
____
____

Day 2: I think ______________________________
____
____

Day 3: I feel ______________________________
____
____

Day 4: I believe ______________________________
____
____

Day 5: My plan is ______________________________
____
____

Day 6: My strategy is ______________________________
____
____

Day 7: My experience is ______________________________
____
____

Live a life where you're ready for anything.

If you live by wisely challenging your limits, you can always embrace opportunities and optimize crises to your benefit.

WEEK 50

Day 1: I understand _______________________________________

____

____

Day 2: I think ____

____

____

Day 3: I feel ____

____

____

Day 4: I believe _______________________________________

____

____

Day 5: My plan is ______________________________________

____

____

Day 6: My strategy is __________________________________

____

____

Day 7: My experience is ________________________________

____

____

Aging is progressive physical deterioration,
don't compound it with your lifestyle.

You can't deny pains or growing a pot belly, but you can do something about them by taking care of yourself.

WEEK 51

Day 1: I understand ___________________________________

____

____

Day 2: I think ___________________________________

____

____

Day 3: I feel ___________________________________

____

____

Day 4: I believe ___________________________________

____

____

Day 5: My plan is ___________________________________

____

____

Day 6: My strategy is ___________________________________

____

____

Day 7: My experience is ___________________________________

____

____

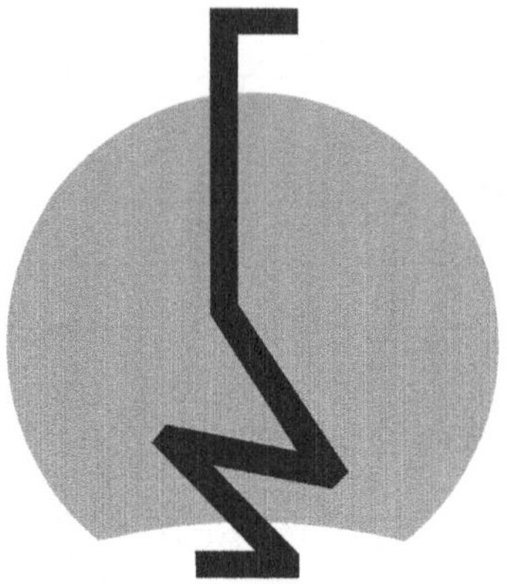

Youthfulness is ageless.

Youthfulness is a collection of qualities we can develop and maintain throughout life, whether we're 8 or 80.

WEEK 52

Day 1: I understand ___________________________________

____

____

Day 2: I think _______________________________________

____

____

Day 3: I feel ____

____

____

Day 4: I believe _____________________________________

____

____

Day 5: My plan is ____________________________________

____

____

Day 6: My strategy is ________________________________

____

____

Day 7: My experience is ______________________________

____

____

ABOUT THE AUTHORS

Aniela and Jerzy Gregorek came to the United States from Poland in 1986 as political refugees during the Solidarity Movement. They both personally knew Jerzy Popieluszko, the priest whose spiritual and emotional support of Warsaw students during the strikes of 1981 and inspiring and tireless work for justice led to his martyrdom in 1984. Jerzy Gregorek was awarded the Medal of Blessed Jerzy Popieluskzko in 2018 for his service in the spirit of truth, love and forgiveness.

Elite professional weightlifters, Jerzy and Aniela have both won multiple world championships and established world records. While working as trainers in L.A., they became aware that people needed a dramatic change in lifestyle, not simply an hour a day of supervised exercise, to achieve real results. The Happy Body Program grew from this insight, supplying definable goals and a plan to sustain improvement. By coaching the UCLA weightlifting team and observing trained athletes, they began to integrate scientific principles to better refine and expand their system.

Today The Happy Body Program has helped thousands of people transform their bodies and lives. Jerzy and Aniela believe that changing character is the most important aspect of the practice, helping people acquire the virtues that make themselves better and improve the planet.

Aniela and Jerzy strive to live virtuous lives on a daily basis with their daughter Natalie in Woodside, California.

Made in the USA
Monee, IL
20 December 2020

54688401R00135